On the Way to Bethlehem
A Child's Storybook for Christmas

written by Daphna Flegal
illustrated by Margaret Lindmark

Published by Abingdon Press.

Copyright © 2011 by Abingdon Press.
All rights reserved.

No part of this work may be reproduced or transmitted in any form or by any means, electronic or mechanical, including photocopying and recording, or by any information storage or retrieval system, except as may be expressly permitted by the 1976 Copyright Act or by permission in writing from the publisher. Requests for permission should be submitted in writing to: Rights and Permissions, The United Methodist Publishing House, 201 Eighth Avenue South, P.O. Box 801, Nashville, TN 37202-0801; faxed to 615-749-6128; or submitted via e-mail to *permissions@abingdonpress.com*.

Scripture quotations noted CEB are from the Common English Bible. Copyright © 2011 by the Common English Bible. All rights reserved. Used by permission.

PACP00936207-01

ISBN 978-1-4267-3616-2

11 12 13 14 15 16 17 18 19 20—10 9 8 7 6 5 4 3 2 1

Abingdon Press • Nashville

Printed in China

Mary walked to the well in the little town of Nazareth. She lowered the small leather bucket until it splashed into the water of the well. Mary pulled up the bucket, now heavy with water. She poured the water into her clay jar. Then she placed the jar on her head, ready to walk back home.

Suddenly, Mary heard a voice.

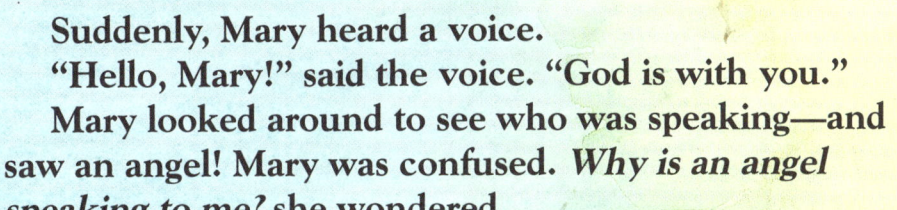

"Hello, Mary!" said the voice. "God is with you."

Mary looked around to see who was speaking—and saw an angel! Mary was confused. *Why is an angel speaking to me?* she wondered.

"Don't be afraid," said the angel. "God has sent me to tell you something wonderful. You will have a baby boy, and you will name him Jesus. He is God's own dear Son."

"How can this happen?" asked Mary. "I'm not married yet."

"Nothing is impossible for God," answered the angel.

"I am God's servant," said Mary humbly. "I'm willing to do what God wants me to do."

Joseph was in the carpenter's shop, making a door. He swung the adze back and forth across a tree trunk to remove the rough bark and leave a clean surface behind. Next, he used a sharp saw to cut the trunk into planks. Sawdust fell to the ground as the saw cut through the wood. Then, he planed the knotty surface of each plank to make it smooth. Finally, he used a mallet to hammer the planks together to make the door the right size.

While he worked, Joseph thought about Mary. Mary was going to have a baby—and they were not married yet. *I don't want to hurt Mary,* he thought. *It will be best to quietly call off the wedding.*

Joseph was still thinking about Mary when night came. He rolled out his sleeping mat and lay down. Even though he was worried, he quickly fell asleep. And as he slept, an angel spoke to Joseph in a dream.

"Joseph," said the angel. "Mary's baby is God's Son. God wants you to marry her. After the baby is born, you will name him Jesus."

When Joseph woke, he knew what he would do. Mary would become his wife, and they would have a baby. The baby's name would be Jesus.

Joseph moved to Nazareth to be with Mary while they waited for the baby to be born.

"Everyone must go to his hometown to be counted," decreed the Emperor Augustus. "Everyone's name must be written on the tax lists."

So even though it was now time for Mary's baby to be born, Mary and Joseph had to go to Bethlehem, Joseph's hometown.

Mary and Joseph packed a donkey with bundles of food, blankets, and the soft cloths needed for the baby. Then they began the long journey from Nazareth to Bethlehem. For ten days, Joseph led Mary and the donkey across the valley and up the mountains. At the end of each day, they stopped where there was water and camped under the stars for the night.

Finally, they arrived in Bethlehem. The little town was crowded with all the people who had come to register for the census. The guest rooms were full. There was no place for Mary and Joseph to stay. So Mary and Joseph went to the stable where animals were kept. There, Joseph made a soft bed for Mary out of hay.

That night God's Son was born. Mary wrapped the baby in soft cloths. Joseph piled clean hay into the feeding trough to make a warm bed for the newborn child. While the animals slept nearby, Mary laid the baby in the sweet-smelling hay. The baby's name was Jesus.

Outside on the hillside, shepherds were watching their sheep. It was late at night, and the shepherds huddled around the campfires to stay warm.

Suddenly, an angel appeared in the sky! A bright light flashed around the shepherds.

"What's happening?" cried the shepherds. "What is that light?" The shepherds covered their eyes and shook with fear.

"Don't be afraid," said the angel. "I have come with a message from God. God's Son is born. You will find him wrapped in soft cloths and lying in a manger."

Suddenly, more and more angels appeared in the sky. "Praise God," sang all the angels. "Praise God in heaven. Peace on earth to everyone." The shepherds were amazed at the beautiful songs.

"Let's go into Bethlehem," said the shepherds. "Let's find this baby lying in a feeding trough for animals."

The shepherds hurried to Bethlehem. They searched the streets of the city until they found the stable. The shepherds quietly entered and knelt among the animals. There they saw the tiny baby lying in a feeding trough, just as the angel said.

"An angel came and told us about your baby," the shepherds told Mary. "And so we have come to see this baby who is God's Son. Praise God!" the shepherds continued. "God's Son is born!" Mary thought about the shepherds' words and held them close in her heart.

START

FINISH

Christmas "To-Do" List

- ❏ Pray for each member of your family.
- ❏ Pray for your teacher.
- ❏ Pray for people who are lonely at Christmas.
- ❏ Pray for persons who are sick at Christmas.
- ❏ Pray for the children of the world.
- ❏ Pray for peace at Christmas and all the time.
- ❏ Wish everyone a Merry Christmas!

November/Noviembre				December/Diciembre		
27	28	29	30	1	2	3
4	5	6	7	8	9	10
11	12	13	14	15	16	17
18	19	20	21	22	23	24
25	26	27	28	29	30	31

And they will call him, Emmanuel.
(*Emmanuel* **means "God with us."**)
Matthew 1:23, CEB